discover evolve prepare research dream

plan succeed explore grow investigate

discover evolve prepare research dream

plan succeed explore grow investigate

discover evolve prepare research dream

plan succeed explore grow investigate

discover evolve prepare research dream

plan succeed explore grow investigate

discover evolve prepare research dream

plan succeed explore grow investigate

discover evolve prepare research dream

plan succeed explore grow investigate

discover evolve prepare research dream

plan succeed explore grow investigate

discover evolve prepare research dream

plan succeed explore grow investigate

CAREER DREAMS

AN ESSENTIAL WORKBOOK FOR
FINDING YOUR PASSION AND PURPOSE

→

Susan Wilson Hulett

Bluestreak
BOOKS

Bluestreak Books is an imprint of Weldon Owen,
a Bonnier Publishing USA company
www.bonnierpublishingusa.com

Edited by Girl Friday Productions
www.girlfridayproductions.com

Designed by Amanda Richmond

Written by Susan Wilson Hulett

Library of Congress Cataloging in Publication data is available.

ISBN-13: 978-1-68188-191-1

Cover images: © Daniiel/Shutterstock; © Vector Market/
Shutterstock; © Janos Levente/Shutterstock

First Printed in 2018

10 9 8 7 6 5 4 3 2 1
2018 2019 2020 2021

Printed in China

↓ INTRODUCTION

If you're holding this book, you're about to embark on a journey. This might inspire all kinds of feelings within you: hopefulness, excitement, or impatience, for example. And you wouldn't be alone if you were also experiencing apprehension, uncertainty, or fear. Having any or all emotions is perfectly natural when venturing into the unknown. Just by beginning this workbook you are making progress—you're saying to yourself, "Yes, I'm ready to open my mind and my heart, to find my truest passions and a career that honors them."

Asking yourself the big questions—such as "What do I want to do with my life? What makes my heart sing?"—can be tough. There are no easy answers, and you're bound to take missteps along the way. That's perfectly natural and fine, and you might just find that what seems to be a detour brings you to a valuable insight you wouldn't have had otherwise.

Whether you're a recent college graduate looking for your first "real" job, a young professional ready for the Next

Big Step, or someone who is going back to work after a hiatus, this journal will help to guide you with thoughtful tips, smart exercises, and wise words from celebrated individuals who've reached for the stars themselves. On these pages, you'll examine the things that make you tick and nurture your soul. You'll discover careers that speak to those unique qualities in you. And finally, you'll put your best foot forward toward launching your first—or next—career. (That's right: there may be *more than* one dream career ahead of you.)

So, get ready to look inward, outward, backward, and ahead. To consult your deepest self, some old friends, and at least a few new acquaintances. Finding the right career is work. But it's worth it, because *you're* worth it. It's your future—get ready to make the most of it.

PART 1

DISCOVER YOUR PASSION
AND PURPOSE IN LIFE

You are the heroes of your story.

—**KERRY WASHINGTON**,
(b. 1977), actor

If you could do anything with the next year of your life, what would it be? It doesn't have to be practical or even realistic—it can be anything.

Describe this vision, and then write down one *quality* of this activity that intrigues and excites you the most. If you're not sure what that quality is, ask yourself: What's the very first word you'd use to describe this activity?

 **TIP**

Understanding the essential

trait that you love about something can
help you to recognize and be open to
other activities—or even careers—
that embody or evoke that trait.

Write a list of things you love doing in your everyday life.

Remember these as you think about possible careers—you may not be able to hike for a living, but perhaps there's a career that allows you to immerse yourself in the natural world, either literally or by contributing to its preservation.

Next to each item, write a short phrase that captures the essence of why you like that activity. For example:

hiking → being close to nature
volunteering → helping people
traveling → encountering new cultures

*

....

....

*

....

....

*

*

*

*

*

*

*

*

*

*

*

*

TIP

Before you find your career,

in many ways you are like a blank slate.
And that's the beauty of this time in
your life: it's full of possibility.

Volunteering is a great way to explore potential passions.

You might be surprised by what you learn while working for free. And it gives you practical experience to put on your résumé and discuss in interviews.

Use the space that follows to brainstorm about some organizations you could contact for volunteer opportunities. Refer back to the activities and traits you uncovered on page 10 to guide you. Feeling stumped? Search a site like VolunteerMatch.org for inspiration.

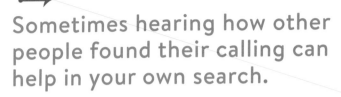

Sometimes hearing how other people found their calling can help in your own search.

Do you know someone who absolutely loves their career? Talk to this person and see what you can learn about their path.

Have more than one person in mind? Turn to pages 160 through 163 for additional room to write.

Write down a few questions you could ask. For example, why do they love their work? Were they surprised to find themselves in this career? Did they ever envision or try something else?

—HOW TO—
LOVE A CAREER

Name of Interviewee

After your conversation, reflect on what
they said. What did they share that might be
useful as you search for your own career?

.

....

....

....

....

....

....

....

....

....

....

TIP

Informational interviews

are a great way to learn about a particular
career path or job. If you feel shy or nervous
about requesting one, remember that
most people have been in your very same
shoes, and just about everyone likes
to talk about themselves!

You carry the passport to your own happiness.

—DIANE VON FURSTENBERG
(b. 1946), fashion designer

Searching for your passion can be hard—and frustrating. It can also be a little frightening.

Sometimes writing about your fears can diminish their power or stop them from interfering with your efforts. Are you experiencing frustrations or roadblocks? Fears or concerns? Write about them here.

TIP

The things that drive you

or bring you peace and contentment don't
have to be glamorous or impressive to
other people. They just have to be the
things that make *you* feel happy or
that *you* find meaningful.

How do you measure "success" in your own life?

Is it about recognition? Monetary reward? Stability and security? Any or all of these are perfectly legitimate, but that doesn't necessarily mean they define success for you.

Think about something you've done that you're truly proud of, something you'd deem a success in your life. What was it, and why did you feel successful? Write about this.

....

....

....

....

....

....

....

....

....

....

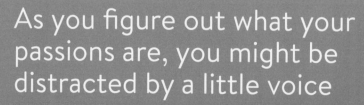

As you figure out what your passions are, you might be distracted by a little voice

(or voices) that tries to devalue your interests or questions the relevance of your efforts to your future career.

It's worth thinking about where this voice might be coming from—a parent, a peer, general conventional "wisdom"—and whether it is worth listening to, or if it's better acknowledging it and then letting go.

What are some of the things that the little voice says to you?

....

....

....

....

....

....

....

....

_____

_____

_____

_____

_____

_____

_____

_____

Is there any merit to what it's saying? What is true, and what might not be?

_____

_____

_____

_____

_____

_____

_____

_____

....

....

....

....

....

....

....

....

What might your counter-response be?

....

....

....

....

....

....

....

....

....

....

....

TIP

You don't have to feel bound

by your past. Perhaps you chose a college
major that no longer resonates, or you followed
someone's advice and things didn't work out.
It's likely those were important learning
experiences—*and* it's OK to change course.

Sometimes, a passion can become clearer when you realize what you're *not* passionate about.

For example, did you always find you had to drag yourself to math class during your school days? A career that involves a lot of bookkeeping or financial forecasting may not be right for you. Do you find that conflict wears you down? Then think twice before considering a career in law or law enforcement.

Write down a list of things that do *not* inspire you.

*

*

*

*

*

*

They say experience is the best teacher.

So talk to someone with lots of it—someone who is retired or near the end of their career. If you want to interview more than one person, use the space on pages 164 through 167.

Write down a few questions to ask them. For example, what did they value most about their working life? Do they have any regrets? What are the most important lessons they learned? And what's their advice for someone like you who is figuring out their career path?

—LESSONS OF—
EXPERIENCE

Name of Interviewee

_____

After your conversation, reflect on what
they said. Did they share any insights
that might be helpful to you?

....

....

....

....

....

....

....

....

....

....

....

PART 2

ENVISION THE CAREER
THAT'S RIGHT FOR YOU

The only way to do great work is to love what you do.

—STEVE JOBS

(1955–2011), cofounder of Apple Computer, Inc.

Have you ever taken a personality test like the classic Myers-Briggs Type Indicator?

These tests can give you valuable insight into your strengths, weaknesses, and what motivates you.

There are lots of free tests online. See page 155 for a possible test site or chose your own. Find one, take the test, and then answer these questions:

Did the test's description of your personality ring true for you? Write about what seemed correct, what didn't, and what surprised you.

Some tests may indicate your working style, the type of leadership you work best under, the sort of roles you like, how you interact with technology, your communication style, and so on. Write down these results here.

Some tests align personality types with particular industries. For access to personality type descriptions and associated career paths, see page 155. What roles or industries does the test indicate you would work best in? Do any of these interest you?

TIP

When searching for a career,

consider all your interests—not just the very top one. For example, if you love cooking but you also love travel, your choices aren't just chef or travel agent. Perhaps you'd be happy as a chef at a multinational resort chain or on a cruise line. Get creative when thinking about all your possibilities.

Go back to the list you made on page 10.

Randomly pair the short phrases that capture the essence of why you like those activities. For example:

helping people / encountering new cultures

Then, list all the professions that each combination brings to mind. For example:

helping people / encountering new cultures: English teacher overseas, international aid worker, foreign service officer

—ACTIVITIES—   —PROFESSION—

....

....

....

....

....

....

—ACTIVITIES—

—PROFESSION—

—ACTIVITIES—

—PROFESSION—

Don't be intimidated by what you don't know.

—SARA BLAKELY

(b. 1971), entrepreneur

The career you're considering—do you know what it's really like?

Think about a day in the life of someone who works in that profession. Write down what you imagine occurs inside that person's typical week, including the highs, the lows, and the mundane.

What are the key responsibilities?

....

....

....

....

....

....

....

....

....

....

....

....

How is a typical day spent? How much time is spent:

In meetings?

....

On the phone?

....

Traveling from place to place?

....

Performing solitary work?

....

Doing "billable" work? (That is, the work we typically associate with the profession. For a doctor, this would mean spending time with a patient; for a lawyer, this would mean meeting with clients or colleagues on a particular case, appearing in court, or doing legal research, etc.)

....

What are the greatest challenges and frustrations each week?

What tasks are most enjoyable?

Do you know anyone in the profession you imagined on page 52?

List their names here, select one, and request an informational interview with them. You'll find room for additional interviews on pages 168 through 171.

Ask them what their typical day is like.

—THE—
THE REALITY OF

_____

Name of Interviewee

_____

After they've told you about their job, show them what
you've written. Does it match their reality? Write about the
similarities and differences from what you imagined.

....

....

....

....

....

....

....

....

....

....

....

TIP

To learn what a particular

profession *feels* like, intern. Even if the
internship doesn't turn into a job, it'll help
you identify what you do and don't like
about the industry and it will give you an
experience you can put on your résumé.

→

Identifying what you've liked or disliked in past experiences can help you as you explore potential careers.

For example, if you enjoy "selling" an idea or product, sales or marketing might appeal to you. If you get satisfaction from building processes and facilitating a team's progress toward a shared goal, you might enjoy being a professional project manager. If you're a gifted communicator who likes describing technology, you might like technical writing.

In the space that follows, write out a list of jobs you've had. On the left, include all the jobs you've held—including full- and part-time jobs, volunteer jobs, and internships or work-study. On the right, write three things you liked and three things you disliked about each.

Once you've completed your list, circle any phrases that are similar.

JOBS	+ LIKES / − DISLIKES
Example: **RECEPTIONIST**	**+** welcoming clients
	+ setting appointments
	+ meeting interesting people
	− dealing with unhappy clients
	− sitting most of the day
	− low pay
	+
	+
	+
	−
	−
	−
	+
	+
	+
	−
	−
	−

JOBS

+ LIKES / − DISLIKES

+ ....
....

+ ....
....

+ ....
....

− ....
....

− ....
....

− ....
....

+ ....
....

+ ....
....

+ ....
....

− ....
....

− ....
....

− ....
....

+ ....
....

+ ....
....

+ ....
....

− ....
....

− ....
....

− ....
....

JOBS

+ LIKES / – DISLIKES

+
+
+
–
–
–
+
+
+
–
–
–
+
+
+
–
–
–

TIP

During this time in your life,

a lot of people may offer advice. And
that can be very helpful. But remember:
everyone has biases, so filter all advice
carefully. Listen with an open mind
and heart—then trust your gut.

As career ideas begin to emerge, you'll want to investigate a few practical considerations.

Knowing these things can help you decide how invested you are in a particular career and get you thinking about the real steps you'll need to take. To get you started, we've listed a few important questions below. Research each one, and write down what you learn.

How much does this career pay for your desired position?

....

....

....

....

How does that compare with your expected living expenses?

....

....

....

....

....

How high does the salary go?

....

....

....

....

....

Is there a lot of travel involved?

....

....

....

....

....

What's required for entry (another degree or some special
training, perhaps)?

....

....

....

....

....

....

Can you think of other considerations? Write the questions and answers here.

Life-fulfilling work is never about the money.

—EILEEN FISHER

(b. 1950), fashion designer

Trying to nail down your career options can be hard—and a little stressful.

Sometimes writing about your stresses can diminish their power and stop them from interfering with your efforts. Maybe you're having trouble narrowing down a bunch of intriguing ideas, or perhaps not even one idea has inspired you.

Are you experiencing stress or doubt? Confusion or exhaustion? Write about it here.

Beware of rationalizing your way into a career. If you catch yourself trying to "talk yourself" into a choice, step back and ask why.

Are you trying to adapt to a career choice that is *someone else's* dream or trying to manufacture enthusiasm for a career that looks good on paper but simply doesn't excite you?

What are some expectations you learned about career goals? What might the source be—a parent, a mentor, your peers, society at large?

....

....

....

....

....

....

....

....

....

Reflect on these expectations. What do you agree
with or believe to be true?

What does not ring true to or resonate with you?

TIP

Remind yourself that

anything is possible. Even when
you run into roadblocks, keep your mind
open and keep going—you truly never
know what's just around the bend.

As you begin your journey toward your best career, know that you might make some wrong turns.

In the end, every experience is valuable—even your mistakes.

Write about a "mistake" you've made in the past that brought new insight or unexpected positive consequences.

....

....

....

....

....

....

....

....

....

....

In the end, what lessons did you learn from the experience?

....

....

....

....

....

....

....

....

....

....

....

....

....

....

....

....

....

....

....

Failure is not the opposite of success, it's an integral part of success.

—**ARIANNA HUFFINGTON**

(b. 1950), cofounder of the HUFFINGTON POST

→ Just because you excel at something doesn't mean it's your calling. Potential isn't the same thing as passion.

You can find a career that involves something that you're both good at *and* that you love.

On the left, make a list of five things you do well. Then, note whether you like this activity, rating from 1 for strongly dislike to 5 for strongly like.

STRENGTHS

1 STRONGLY DISLIKE 2 DISLIKE
3 NEUTRAL 4 LIKE 5 STRONGLY LIKE

Example:

I'm good at organization.

4

1. ....

   .... ☐

2. ....

   .... ☐

3. ....

   .... ☐

4. ....

   .... ☐

5. ....

   .... ☐

PART 3

FOLLOW YOUR DREAM

I learned a long time ago that there is something worse than missing the goal, and that's not pulling the trigger.

—MIA HAMM

(b. 1972), professional soccer player

Now that you've done the hard work of narrowing down your career options, you're ready for the next step.

If you've made a choice that requires some formal schooling, you'll want to bookmark this section for now. If not, take a deep breath and get ready to find—and land—that first job along your professional path. Let's start with a powerful tool: networking.

Create a list of five people who are connected to a job you want or a company you think you'd like to work for.

1. ....

2. ....

3. ....

4. ....

5. ....

Now contact these people with the goal of scheduling at least three informational interviews. Take notes for each, and write down any insights, advice, or new contact leads you might want to reach out to down the road. Do you need additional space? See pages 172 through 175.

—INTERVIEW—
#1

Name of Interviewee

_____

—INTERVIEW—
#**2**

Name of Interviewee

_____

—INTERVIEW—
#**3**

Name of Interviewee

_____

TIP

Be careful not to put too

much pressure on the first few jobs in
your career journey. No one starts at
the top. Some jobs will be stepping-
stones—and that's just fine.

→

Who you work with and a company's day-to-day culture can be as important as the job you do. Think about your ideal workplace culture.

WORKPLACE WISH LIST

What are the qualities you most want to find?
For example, room for growth, work-life balance,
flexible scheduling, parental leave, an easy commute,
or a pet-friendly office.

....

....

....

....

....

....

....

....

WORKPLACE DEAL BREAKERS

What are the qualities you want to avoid? Think about things such as low workplace morale, limited vertical promotions, or excessive travel.

TIP

What are some ways you

can determine whether a job has any of
these qualities? Beyond the company's stated
policies and your gut instincts, you might also
be able to glean some knowledge at industry
mixers or networking events. Websites like
glassdoor.com and indeed.com, which offer
salary information and employee reviews
of companies, can also be helpful.

Let's take our networking to the next level.

You've reached out to individuals—now it's time to contact some helpful organizations.

List three organizations that might be helpful in your job search. Think: alumni organizations, professional associations, and so on.

1. ....

2. ....

3. ....

Research any upcoming events these organizations are hosting in your area, with the goal of getting at least one item placed on your calendar in the next month. Turn to pages 155 and 156 for a list of organizations to get you started.

At or after attending the event, write down any new contacts, insights, or advice. Need additional space? See pages 176 through 179.

—EVENT—
#1

—EVENT—
#2

—EVENT—
#3

Never be so
faithful to your
plan that you
are unwilling to
consider the
unexpected.

—**ELIZABETH WARREN**
(b. 1949), US senator

TIP

Before you put yourself out

there as a job seeker or intern candidate, remember that you're already out there on social media. Anything the public can see on Facebook, Instagram, and Twitter will be seen by the people you reach out to. So, clean up those pages and triple-check your privacy settings. And be sure to post on or update your LinkedIn profile with recommendations from past jobs or internships you've had.

Go through each work experience and accomplishment you list on your résumé and prepare to elaborate on it during interviews and calls with recruiters.

To help, write out the answers to the questions below. As your career journey progresses and you have new experiences to consider, return to this exercise using page 184.

What were some of your greatest successes? How did you achieve them?

Are there gaps in your employment or education history? If so, can you explain them?

What is it about your skills and experience that make you the best person for this job?

TIP

Résumés and cover letters

are not one-type-fits-all. When applying
for a job, read the description carefully.
Does your résumé demonstrate the
required skills? If not, make adjustments
and use key terms from the job posting.
As for your cover letter, don't restate your
entire résumé—be more targeted in
your approach. This is your time to
stand out, with professionalism
and personality.

Before an interview, do your homework about the company.

Do you have interviews scheduled at more than one company?

Turn to pages 180 through 183 for additional writing space.

Research as much as you can about the company, the position, and the people you'll be interviewing with. Write all your findings down here.

Write down a few insightful questions to ask about the company. For example, what's their greatest challenge? And how might your role be involved in overcoming that challenge? This will show that you're prepared, interested, and engaged.

═══ TIP ═══

Nervous about interviewing?

Nothing beats the jitters like plenty
of practice. Role-play a few interviews
with friends. Or, better yet, go big and join a
public speaking group, such as Toastmasters.
The more you stare down the thing that
scares you, the less powerful it becomes.

Interviewers often ask about challenges you've had and how you've overcome them.

Think about past jobs, class projects, or volunteer tasks you've worked on, and write out your answers to the questions below.

Which ones presented the greatest challenges to you
and why?

How did you solve those challenges?

If faced with any one of those challenges again, is there anything you would do differently? Is there anything you would do the same way?

═ TIP ═

Job interviewing is a little
like dating—never trash your ex on a
first date. Even if you're asked about past
challenges in the workplace, be careful and
diplomatic when discussing the part a
former manager or coworker played.
Negativity and blame, even if they're
deserved, make the wrong first impression.

Think about your greatest weakness and how it might present an opportunity for growth.

Make a list of three of your weaknesses. For example, do you sometimes try to take on too much? Do you occasionally get too fixated when working on a difficult problem?

1. ....

....

....

2. ....

....

....

3. ....

....

....

Which of these is your *greatest* weakness? Circle it.

Has this tendency affected your work in the past, either in school or at a job? If so, how?

Now, think about how you can manage this weakness. For example, if you tend to take on too much, could you find ways to delegate tasks or better monitor your workload? Write about some potential strategies here.

....

....

....

....

....

....

....

....

....

....

....

....

....

....

....

....

....

THE INTERVIEW CHECKLIST

AT LEAST ONE DAY BEFORE YOUR INTERVIEW:

- ☐ Confirm the date, time, and location of the interview.

- ☐ Choose and prepare your interview outfit.

- ☐ Print extra copies of your résumé and reference list.

- ☐ Pack a small notebook and a pen (plus an extra).

- ☐ Download directions to the interview site and information about parking (if you'll be driving to the interview).

- ☐ Research traffic along your route at the appropriate time of day and plan your departure so you'll get to the interview early.

- ☐ Make sure you have enough gas in your car (if you'll be driving to the interview).

ON THE DAY OF, BE SURE YOU HAVE YOUR:

- ☐ Résumé and references
- ☐ Notebook and pen
- ☐ Bag or briefcase
- ☐ Directions
- ☐ Phone ringer turned to silent

After each interview, write a short thank-you note on professional stationery.

In most cases e-mail is also fine—especially if you're interviewing with a technology company or the hiring manager is making a final decision very soon. The most important thing is to send something right away. Write your first draft on the pages that follow.

THANK-YOU CHECKLIST

BEFORE YOU MAIL YOUR

THANK-YOU NOTE OR HIT "SEND":

☐ Make sure you spelled the recipient's name correctly.

☐ If you state the recipient's position at the company, confirm it against their website or business card.

☐ Express your thanks for their time and consideration.

☐ Consider mentioning a specific part of the interview that you felt was particularly enlightening. Or perhaps write about an aspect of the job that excites you and how you think your skills and passions would be a good match for it.

☐ Let them know you'll look forward to hearing from them soon (or whenever they indicated the next step would take place or a hiring decision would be made).

If you're not happy with how

an interview went—perhaps you were
nervous or didn't answer questions as well
as you could have—don't beat yourself up.
Reflect on what went wrong, think
about how you can do better next time,
then forgive yourself and move on.

If you've had a bad or so-so interview, use the experience to help you refine your interviewing techniques.

To repeat this exercise following additional interviews, go to page 186.

Where did you fall flat? Where did you shine?

....

....

....

....

....

....

....

....

....

....

....

Did the interviewer ask you questions you weren't expecting? Write those here, and then answer them.

Use this space to map out a strategy for doing better next time. For example, consider whether you thought about your skills as they relate to the job beforehand. Did you come prepared with examples of your successes in the workplace and how you've handled challenges? Could you research the next company you interview with more extensively?

You just have to keep doing something, seizing the next opportunity, staying open to trying something new.

—SHONDA RHIMES
(b. 1970), writer, producer, and author of Year of Yes:
How to Dance It Out, Stand In the Sun, and Be Your Own Person

TIP

If you find yourself nervous

during an interview, try this trick:
Sit up straight, take a deep breath, and
focus for a moment on the feeling of the
chair beneath you. Think about how it's
supporting you; feel it holding you up so
you can face this situation. Then think
about the floor under the chair and the earth
under the floor. All of these things are
there to support you; that focus on "support"
can have a positive psychological effect.

Once you've done a couple of job or informational interviews, think back to the values and priorities you identified on page 98.

Which are most important to you now? Are they the same as before? Or different?

Which are the least important to you now? Are they the same or different?

Job searching can be tough work. It requires staying positive in the face of rejection.

Feeling weary or frustrated is perfectly natural.

If you need to vent a little, use the space that follows to write down all the things that are frustrating you.

Careers are a jungle gym, not a ladder.

—SHERYL SANDBERG

(b. 1969), CEO of Facebook and author of
Lean In: Women, Work, and the Will to Lead

≡ TIP ≡

Once you get that first job on
your dream career path, take a moment to
congratulate yourself. You've worked hard and
achieved something amazing. There are more
steps ahead—promotions and new jobs, some
that are along a straight line toward your goal,
and some that are less so. And of course as
you grow and change, your career choice may
change too. Tuck this book away somewhere
handy—because your journey isn't over yet.

HELPFUL RESOURCES

TO FIND VOLUNTEER OPPORTUNITIES
VolunteerMatch.org • Volunteers of America: voa.org
Peace Corps: peacecorps.gov

TO PRACTICE PUBLIC SPEAKING
(helpful for combatting interview jitters):
Toastmasters International: toastmasters.org

TO EXPLORE YOUR STRENGTHS, LIKES, AND DISLIKES
Take the Myers-Briggs Type Indicator test:
16personalities.com

FOR PERSONALITY TYPE DESCRIPTIONS AND ASSOCIATED CAREER STRENGTHS
16personalities.com/personality-types

TO TEST YOUR KNOWLEDGE AND LEARN MORE ABOUT CAREERS
Mycareerquizzes.com

TO EXPLORE CONTINUING EDUCATION AND SKILL DEVELOPMENT
Lynda.com

HELPFUL RESOURCES

For job listings, company reviews, salary information, professional advice, networking opportunities, and more

- LinkedIn.com • Glassdoor.com • Indeed.com
- USAJobs.gov • Nationalcareerfairs.com
- The Muse: themuse.com
- Payscale: payscale.com
- Career Contessa: careercontessa.com
- Levo: levo.com
- Summit Series: summit.co
- Founders Society: foundersociety.co
- National Association of Professional Women: napw.com
- Young Entrepreneur Council: yec.co
- Business Networking International: bni.com
- National Association of Environmental Professionals: naep.org

SUGGESTED READING

BIG MAGIC
Creative Living Beyond Fear
Elizabeth Gilbert

LEAN IN
Women, Work, and the Will to Lead
Sheryl Sandberg

ORIGINALS
How Non-Conformists Move the World
Adam Grant

THE ARTIST'S WAY
A Spiritual Path to Higher Creativity
Julia Cameron

POUR YOUR HEART INTO IT
How Starbucks Built a Company One Cup at a Time
Howard Schultz

SUGGESTED READING

WHAT YOU PRACTICE IS WHAT YOU HAVE
A Guide to Having the Life You Want
Cheri Huber

THE TIPPING POINT
How Little Things Can Make a Big Difference
Malcolm Gladwell

DESIGNING YOUR LIFE
How to Build a Well-Lived, Joyful Life
Bill Burnett and Dave Evans

THE ANTI 9-TO-5 GUIDE
Practical Career Advice for Women
Who Think Outside the Cube
Michelle Goodman

#GIRLBOSS
Sophia Amoruso

—ADDITIONAL—
WORKSPACE

Here you can find extra worksheets to log fresh insight
from informational interviews and networking events,
and more space for job interview research and reflection.
Because finding a career you love is an ongoing
journey, and these pages are here to help you grow.

If you know someone who absolutely loves their career, talk to them and see what you can learn about their journey.

Write down a few questions you could ask.

—HOW TO—
LOVE A CAREER

Name of Interviewee

_____

What did they share that might be useful as
you search for your own career?

....
....
....
....
....
....
....
....
....
....
....
....

If you know someone who absolutely loves their career, talk to them and see what you can learn about their journey.

Write down a few questions you could ask.

—HOW TO—
LOVE A CAREER

Name of Interviewee

_____

What did they share that might be useful as
you search for your own career?

....
....
....
....
....
....
....
....
....
....
....
....

Ask someone who is retired or near the end of their career what they've learned from their experience.

Write down a few questions to ask them.

....
....
....
....
....
....
....
....
....
....
....
....
....

—LESSONS OF—
EXPERIENCE

Name of Interviewee

_____

Did they share any insights that might be
helpful during your career search?

....

....

....

....

....

....

....

....

....

....

....

Ask someone who is retired or near the end of their career what they've learned from their experience.

Write down a few questions to ask them.

—LESSONS OF—
EXPERIENCE

Name of Interviewee

_____

Did they share any insights that might be
helpful during your career search?

....

....

....

....

....

....

....

....

....

....

....

Do you know what the career you're considering is really like?

Talk to someone who has your ideal job. Write down what you imagine occurs inside that person's typical week. Then ask them what an average day looks like.

....

....

....

....

....

....

....

....

....

....

....

....

....

....

—THE—
REALITY OF

_____

Name of Interviewee

_____

Does what you imagined match their reality?

....

....

....

....

....

....

....

....

....

....

....

Do you know what the career you're considering is really like?

Talk to someone who has your ideal job. Write down what you imagine occurs inside that person's typical week. Then ask them what an average day looks like.

—THE—
REALITY OF

_____

Name of Interviewee

_____

Does what you imagined match their reality?

....

....

....

....

....

....

....

....

....

....

....

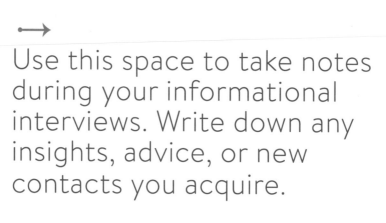

Use this space to take notes during your informational interviews. Write down any insights, advice, or new contacts you acquire.

—INTERVIEW—
#1

Name of Interviewee

_____

—INTERVIEW—
#2

Name of Interviewee

_____

—INTERVIEW—
#3

Name of Interviewee

_____

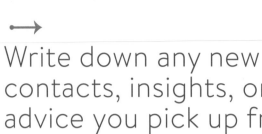

Write down any new
contacts, insights, or
advice you pick up from your
networking events.

—EVENT—
#1

—EVENT—
#2

—EVENT—
#3

Heading out on another interview?

Do your homework about the company before you do.

—COMPANY NAME—

Research as much as you can about the company, the position, and the people you'll be interviewing with. Write your findings down here.

Write down a few insightful questions to ask about the company.

Heading out on another interview?

Do your homework about the company before you do.

—COMPANY NAME—

Research as much as you can about the company, the position, and the people you'll be interviewing with. Write your findings down here.

Write down a few insightful questions to ask about
the company.

Have you updated your résumé recently?

Prepare to elaborate on your new work experiences or accomplishments during interviews and calls with recruiters. To help, write out the answers to the questions below.

What important skill or insight have you gained from this new experience?

How will this new skill or insight improve your ability to do this job?

Had another
less-than-ideal interview?

That's OK—practice makes perfect. Use the experience to help you refine your interviewing techniques.

Where did you fall flat? Where did you shine?

....

....

....

....

....

....

....

....

....

....

....

....

....

....

Did the interviewer ask you questions you weren't
expecting? Write those here, and then answer them.

Use this space to map out a strategy for doing better next time.

ABOUT THE AUTHOR

SUSAN WILSON HULETT has spent the past twenty-plus years exploring a range of career options. A licensed attorney, Susan took her first "real" job after law school as an English teacher in Pusan, South Korea. After that, she took on the role of managing editor at a travel magazine based in Seattle, Washington, followed by several other jobs in print media. She's also worked for Microsoft and, most recently, Girl Friday Productions, as a production and book editor. She loves adventuring throughout the working world almost as much as she loves traveling to new places. And she never, ever wants to stop pursuing her career dreams.

discover evolve prepare research dream

plan succeed **explore** grow investigate

discover **evolve** prepare research dream

plan succeed explore grow **investigate**

discover evolve **prepare** research dream

plan **succeed** explore grow investigate

discover evolve prepare **research** dream

plan succeed explore **grow** investigate

discover **evolve** prepare research dream

plan succeed explore grow **investigate**

discover evolve **prepare** research dream

plan **succeed** explore grow investigate

discover evolve prepare research **dream**

plan succeed **explore** grow investigate

discover evolve prepare research dream

plan succeed explore **grow** investigate